Northern California's

Best Family Campgrounds

Northern California's Best Family Campgrounds

50 Fun, Affordable, Kid-Friendly Sites

By Roland De Wolk

Photographs by John Swain

CHRONICLE BOOKS

SAN FRANCISCO

Dedication

For roaring campfires that will never be as bright as her eyes,
for mountaintops that will never soar as high as her intelligence,
for blazing summer days that can never hope to be as warm as her heart,
I dedicate all this and all that I am to my Carlita.

Printed in Hong Kong.

Library of Congress Cataloging-in-Publication Data:
  De Wolk, Roland, 1953–
     Northern California's best family campgrounds : 50 fun, affordable, kid-friendly sites /
  by Roland De Wolk ; photographs by John Swain.
       p.   cm.
     Includes index.
     ISBN 0-8118-1270-7 (pbk.)
      1. Camp sites, facilities, etc.—California, Northern—Guidebooks.
  2. Camping—California, Northern—Guidebooks. 3. California, Northern—Guidebooks. I. Title
  GV191.42.C2D4   1997
  796.54'09794—dc20   96–27809
                                            CIP

Cover design: Laura Lovett
Book design and composition: Poulson/Gluck Design
Cover photograph: China Camp State Park by John Swain

Distributed in Canada by Raincoast Books,
8680 Cambie Street
Vancouver BC V6P 6M9

10 9 8 7 6 5 4 3 2 1

Chronicle Books
85 Second Street
San Francisco, CA 94105
Web Site: www.chronbooks.com

Contents

Introduction

Northern California is a part of the world that truly has no rival. And lucky for us, it has the best roads in the whole world to see it. And you have a car that fits right on top of those roads.

Tell me if this also fits: You want to take a road trip and actually experience the great Golden State. You want to motor to the Ventana Wilderness and see the real Big Sur. You want to finally drive through that huge redwood tree off the Redwood Highway and sleep in an ancient redwood forest. You want to be able to stay for the sunset at Tahoe and then spend the night watching shooting stars over those vast, pure waters high in the Sierra Nevada.

And more than that, you want to do all these completely cool and wonderful things with the people you love most: your family.

But there are one or two matters you have to settle first: Money might be one of them. Big Sur, for example. Do you know how much it costs to stay at an inn or cabin around the Big Sur area? For just a couple, a night and three meals can easily cost several hundred dollars. No kidding.

And then there's the deeper question: Do you want to simply see your planet from a window—or do you want to come alive and take your rightful place in your own natural world?

California—from the high Sierra to the blue Pacific, from giant sequoias to deep desert—is not a virtual reality experience. It is arguably the most spectacular stretch of planet any of us can ever experience. You want—you need—to actually be part of it. Not removed from it.

Let's stay with Big Sur for a moment longer.

This book will show you and tell you where you and your family can actually spend the weekend on the beach there, roasting marshmallows, riding bikes and strolling the sands for $3 a night. OK, $5 if you add the marshmallows. Some of the most spectacular places in this book are actually free.

There are 49 more places to choose from ahead of you, places to dream about—and then actually experience.

We have cherry-picked the best for you and your family. We have combed through hundreds of outdoor California spots, traveled across thousands of miles of California roads. And we've eaten a lot of marshmallows.

Join us for a journey at your pace, at your discretion and for your pure pleasure in being a true part of our California.

Every summer, my mom used to say with lots of enthusiasm, "C'mon! Let's go camping!" My dad would always say, with not so much gusto, "I camped enough during the war."

For a lot of folks like my dad, camping has meant two hours setting up a drafty tent, funky food and an uncomfortable night on the cold ground. And you weren't allowed to shoot the enemy, which was usually some drunk at a nearby campsite with a really loud radio.

In case you've been spending too much time at work or in chat rooms on the Net and have lost contact with real reality, this is just in: Things have changed.

Roomy, warm tents take two to five minutes to pop up. Alfresco dining is now four-star. Sleeping gear is toasty and soft. And Sony invented the Walkman.

We're providing you a short list of what you need—and what you might want—to make your 21st century camping excursion the best time ever on the road. Starting from scratch, we can get you going for less than a weekend at an average motel with an average restaurant. And this is stuff you get to keep and use again and again.

A couple of ground rules for this book: With a few notable exceptions, we list places to go car camping. That is, places you drive right up or real close to. Not back-packing sites that require a stiff hike with all your equipment in tow. Almost every site is good for tents and RVs, and when they're not, we'll tell you so. Virtually every road is paved, so you can get there with everything from a 4X4 to a sports car. Just about every place in the book has running water, most have hot showers and all have clean bathroom facilities. If there are exceptions, we note them.

We favor places like national and state parks. Private campgrounds are often pretty dreky. And much more expensive.

Our recommendations are based on key factors: excellence of the location, safety, lots of good, private space between sites and cleanliness (including the bathrooms) of the campground. We also considered the crowd. If there are kids with bikes gently wheeling around, that's good. If there are bums drinking out of gallon bottles of cheap wine they also use as pillows, that's bad. No apologies.

One last note for the skeptical: If you've never gone camping, and always won-dered why so many do—or if you've always wanted to camp, but didn't know where to start, this is especially for you.

C'mon! Let's go camping!

And now an important word about reserving your campsite...

Camping has become much more popular as baby boomers have their own babies. Some campgrounds are filled months in advance. On busy days, several thousand calls are made every hour to the reservation numbers. Summer Fridays and Saturdays are the busiest—and most expensive—by far. Be very sure you call well ahead and get your name on the books.

The national parks generally go through Destinet at 800-365-2267. Destinet also books California state parks, at a separate number: 800-444-7275. For many places you can now make reservations up to seven months in advance. Most national forest sites are first-come, first-served. Local agencies are all different.

The fees cited in this book are usually the highest charged at peak times such as summer weekends. There are generally significant discounts for the elderly, disabled and for veterans.

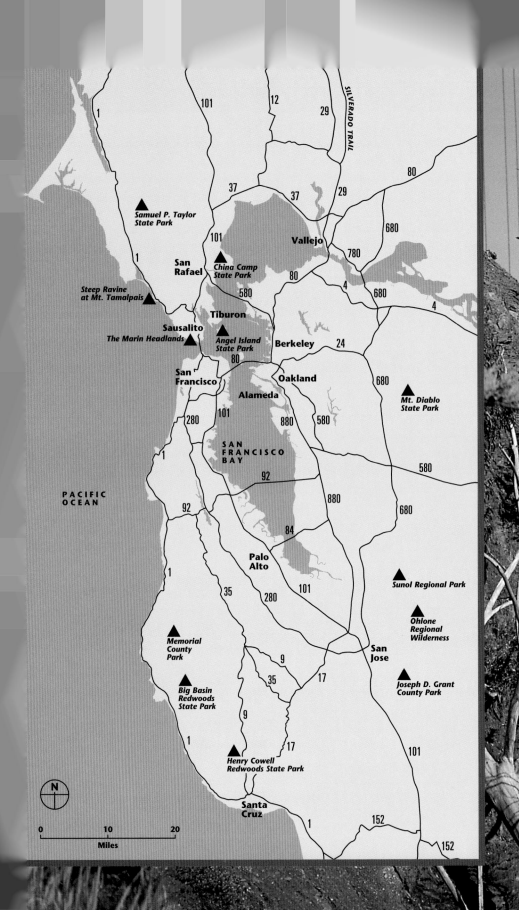

Angel Island State Park

I can say with conviction that you will never be bored on Angel Island. And best of all, hardly anyone knows you can spend the night there. The nine campsites are well hidden in the trees and no one's going out of their way to point them out. In fact, they're not even mentioned in the park brochure.

This is one of the rare places we're sending you that requires you to get out of your car and hoof it into camp. But don't worry, it's about as hard as walking through a shopping center with no escalators. If you've never backpacked more than a baby through a supermarket, this is for you.

There are no cars on Angel Island, except for a ranger vehicle here and there. You take a short, splashy ferry ride across the waters of San Francisco Bay, and get off at the dock. Then you have a 30-minute hike to camp. It's all part of an adventure you cannot find anywhere else.

Angel Island is a 740-acre state park once owned and operated by the military. The remnants of their occupation are everywhere, from deep concrete bunkers to sand-colored shells of buildings left open and ready for hours and hours of exploration. There are wide-open fields of green where the troops would gather for drills. Today, those military parade grounds are used for softball, frisbee and picnics. You may just want to do some cartwheels.

My favorite place is the remains of Fort McDowell, a veritable ghost town left quite open for exploration. You could easily spend the entire day roaming through these beautiful sunwashed ruins along the Bay.

There is also a dark side to Angel Island. The government kept many legal immigrants here for months, sometimes years, ostensibly to be sure they were not carrying infectious diseases. Asian immigrants—especially Chinese—were singled out for much of the first half of this century. There is a common lore that the military kept Japanese Americans here during World War II in a sort of concentration camp. This is not true.

On the sunny side, there is Quarry Beach, all but hidden on the southeast end of the island. It is small, but very sandy and protected from stiff winds.

Perhaps the single biggest attraction is Angel Island's view of San Francisco and beyond from the northern and western ends of the island. I think I've seen the Bay Area from every viewpoint imaginable over many years and yet, I cannot say any are more stunning than those from this green and gold jewel in the Bay.

If you are a bike rider or use a wheelchair to get around, Angel Island is surprisingly friendly. There is a wide, paved road around the park, as well as more rugged and less accessible dirt roads and paths crisscrossing the island at just about every point.

▲ ANGEL ISLAND STATE PARK

The most regular ferry service to Angel Island is from the Marin County town of Tiburon. Call 415-435-2131 for detailed schedule information. There is also summer ferry service from San Francisco (800-229-2784), Oakland and Alameda (510-522-3300) and Vallejo (707-643-3779). For campground reservations, call 800-444-7275. Camping costs $16 a night. Open year-round.

The Marin Headlands

If there is a more spectacular urban place to spend an outdoor weekend than Kirby Cove just beneath the towers of the Golden Gate Bridge, I don't know of it. In fact, I'm having trouble even imagining one. And still more incredible, it's absolutely free.

There are four generous campsites here. I suggest sites two, three and four if you have very young children because they are far from any cliffs.

If your kids are, say, older than 10, my humble advice for a truly tip-top experience is getting a reservation for site number one. From here you can see the towers of the bridge right ahead and the city on the other side of the gate. You can barbecue by the glow of sunset on the orange towers, fall asleep to the sound of waves crashing below, and wake to the sun pouring through the cables. The sound of the distant foghorns is an extra bonus, as if you could ask for more.

But more there is.

The campsites all have slightly elevated pads of sand to set your tent on. Or maybe you just want to sleep under the stars. Either way, a bed of sand is one of my favorite ways to drop into an eight-hour trance.

Each site will hold up to 10 people and you all can stay for up to three days. Make a party of it.

Bring your own wood and water along with whatever else you need or want. Many people bring bikes and running shoes.

Kirby Cove is located in the Marin Headlands, one of the military's spectacular gifts to our generation. There are countless miles of world-class trails above the Bay and Pacific.

Kids will love the empty concrete bunkers, great for climbing and exploring. Watch the flocks of pelicans wing their way out the Golden Gate to sea. Or the cargo ships dieseling into port. The fog rolls in, burns off and rolls in again.

On full moon nights, you can take a tour of the newly restored lighthouse at nearby Point Bonita, right at the mouth of the Golden Gate. Daytime tours are available on a regular basis.

(P.S. If Kirby Cove is filled you could try Bicentennial Camp up the road a bit. There are two small sites sheltered by cypress trees, which also, unfortunately, hide the Golden Gate Bridge from view. I suggest you get a couple of families together and reserve both sites. Otherwise, it's a little too cozy to share with strangers.)

▲ THE MARIN HEADLANDS

To get there from San Francisco go over the Golden Gate
Bridge and take the Alexander Avenue exit off U.S. 101
past Vista Point. Coming from the north, take the second
Sausalito exit just before the bridge. Follow the signs up
the hill into Fort Baker. The first landmark you will see
on the left, overlooking the bridge, will be Battery Spencer.
Just a few yards past that you will see a gate and a road
that will take you to Kirby Cove Campground. For reservations, call the Golden Gate National Recreation Area at
415-331-1540 between 9:30 A.M. and 12 noon. You must
call no sooner than 90 days in advance. No charge.
Camping from April 1 to November 1.

Samuel P. Taylor State Park

This is a true flat-out favorite for thousands of people. And as Point Reyes National Seashore's marvels have become better known over the last 10 years, thousands of people driving out to the coast have seen Samuel P. Taylor State Park and stopped to camp.

It is truly a little community in the height of the summer season. Well-loved campgrounds that draw a loyal population every year have a certain ancient, even atavistic, quality to them.

There are no fences, the homes are paper thin and everyone is privy to everyone else's business. But since you're there for just a few days, that really means instant connections with your neighbors, who probably also have kids, and a holiday atmosphere, which means no one really cares.

Sam Taylor is in a fine grove of second-growth redwoods, where you are far enough inland to get a lot of sun but far enough west to get pure Pacific breezes.

If you take the popular Pioneer Trail, you'll also pass under some virgin redwood stands that escaped Mr. Taylor's 19th-century lumber and paper mill.

Ole Sam bought this land in the Gold Rush days for $5,000 and his paper mill was the first one on the West Coast. You can see the remains of the mill's stone foundation about a mile away from the picnic grounds. And as a bit of historical trivia, you may be amused to know that this is where the square-bottomed paper bag was invented.

Sam Taylor also ran a resort here in the 1870s, a big lodge called the Hotel Azalea, which, like many 19th-century wooden buildings in California, burned to the ground.

In 1946 the land became a state park and ours to enjoy forever.

▲ SAMUEL P. TAYLOR STATE PARK

From Highway 101 in Marin County, get off at the central San Rafael exit, and go west on Fourth Street until it turns into Sir Francis Drake Boulevard. After about another dozen miles you will see the park entrance to your left. Call 800-444-7275 for camping reservations. Please note that this is one of the most popular places to stay in California and is booked solid all summer. It costs $16 a night to camp here. Camping season is year-round.

China Camp State Park

This may be the single most perfect place to run for a night out of the suburbs or city.

Located just north of San Rafael, China Camp is close, has a great historical site and beach on the Bay and an absolutely lovely campground that very often has spaces open.

The campsites are under a generous forest of bay laurels, which send off a fragrance in the afternoon heat you won't forget soon. It fades only at twilight, when the aromas of wood campfires begin to sift through the air. You look up and see the turquoise waters of the Bay just past the deep green of a saltwater marsh.

A broad creek runs through China Camp. It's still running in the spring but dries up in the summer. Which is good, because that means few mosquitos.

The sites are well spaced. The bathroom facilities don't have flush toilets or hot showers, but they are clean and quite adequate. There is piped-in water.

I always bring my baseball mitt and several baseballs when we camp to play catch with my family. I was happy to see others doing the same in the late afternoon the last time I was there.

The number one attraction away from the campground is the old shrimping village just down the road. You can see where Chinese immigrants settled many years ago to fish and live off the abundant waters of the Bay. And if you are very lucky, the super cool old-fashioned lunch counter may be open for business. The hours are irregular, but your best bet is between 10 A.M. and 5 P.M. on weekends. This unnamed artifact is your basic hard-to-find time warp that serves hot dogs, cokes and beers in a pre–World War II atmosphere. Be sure to check out the ancient cigarette machine in the corner.

In good weather, the beach is a great place to swim; in my opinion, it's the best Bay swim spot in the entire region. One more word: You don't drive your car right to the camping spot here; you park in the lot and walk anywhere from 30 to 100 yards in. That makes things even more quiet and safe.

▲ CHINA CAMP
STATE PARK

Off U.S. Highway 101 in San Rafael, take the central San Rafael exit and go straight through the intersection to Third Street. Turn east on Third and head out of town about five miles. The road will turn north along the Bay, which is when it's time to start looking for the signs for China Camp. The old shrimp-fishing village will be on your right. The campground is farther up, less than three miles on your left. Call 800-444-7275 for camping reservations. The cost is $16 a night. Camping is year-round.

Steep Ravine at Mt. Tamalpais

Marin's mountain is huge and varied and immensely popular. It rises up from near the Bay on the east and gives up only when it descends into the ocean to the west.

At the end of a steep slope off Highway 1, just south of Stinson Beach, a small promontory juts out to sea. The park people call it a "marine terrace." Thousands of people who drive north from the city along the highway pass the small gate and road leading to Steep Ravine, not knowing that on their way to hopes of a rustic weekend on the sea, they have passed one of the best hideaways in California.

At the bottom of the steep ravine to the Pacific there is a campground where tidy dome tents fold in nicely with the sea and land. A copse of cypress trees shelter many of the campsites for folks who want an extra measure of protection.

There is a pebbly beach nearby, intense outcroppings of rock that climb right to the top of the mountain and wildflowers that would make a bumblebee quiver.

You will need reservations for this spot, so plan well ahead. You'll get a combination to the gate lock, so you don't have to haul your stuff down to the campsite on foot. Instead, you unlock the gate, coast down a bit of well-tended pavement and unload.

Some people with very young children may feel uncomfortable here, because of the rocky bluffs. Personally, I think a well-cared-for child will profit from the adventure.

(There are also 10 rustic, primitive cabins at the site. You can rent those as well for a very reasonable price.)

The drive to the top of Mt. Tamalpais is a great Bay Area road trip, and the final short hike to the rocky peak is a must. There are more than 50 miles of incredible trails on the mountain.

▲ STEEP RAVINE AT MT. TAMALPAIS

This is a small campground, with just six sites. That's great if you have reservations, which you get by calling 800-444-7275. The gate is easy to miss off Highway 1, so when you're one mile south of Stinson Beach, go slowly. Look for the gate and small sign on the west side of the road. It costs $9 a night to camp here. Open year-round.

STEEP RAVINE AT MT. TAMALPAIS

Big Basin Redwoods State Park

Maybe you are one of the many people who think all the big redwoods in Northern California are far from the Bay Area. Wrong. The Santa Cruz Mountains have lush forests of our most beautiful trees, reaching for the stars above and forming fairy rings below. Most are second growth, because the Bay Area's early logging industry pretty much sliced through all the ancient trees. But because of the ideal growing conditions between the ridges of the San Francisco Peninsula and the beaches of the Pacific, they have grown back remarkably well.

Big Basin is the oldest park in the state's outstanding collection of public lands. It is also perhaps the single most accessible and varied place to get into the middle of these almost magical trees. The rangers know this and have created a small, first-rate museum that explains just about everything from the mystique of the redwoods to their value as lumber. The kids' ranger talks at night around the campfire are outstanding.

And of course, there are the trees themselves. Healthy streams and brooks run through the forests of Big Basin, creating two notable waterfalls and leading the way for strolls through the woods you may never forget.

The one everybody comes to see is Berry Falls, which requires a hike of a little more than five miles from the park headquarters. When you get there, you'll also see lots of visitors from just about every country and continent. Big Basin is very popular, with over a million visitors every year. Fortunately, Big Basin is also, well, very big. It covers more than 16,000 acres and has 80 miles of trails. You can find a great deal of solitude in this land and also connect seamlessly with many other Peninsula parks.

My favorite walk is a full 13-mile hike that starts at Skyline Boulevard on the ridge top, enters Big Basin, and follows the creek right to the sea at Waddell State Beach. The campgrounds at the bottom of the trail are my favorites, but require a good hike.

There are dozens of much more modest but rewarding hikes to suit all pleasures. Check with the rangers at the visitor center. That's why we pay them.

For car camping, any of the sites in the main part of the park are great—and don't pay too much attention to the qualifications of the so-called "environmental" sites—which is eco-jargon for having to hike in and have no water or flush toilets right there.

The environmental sites at Big Basin are very close to the parking lot, the bathrooms and even the store.

One last note: If you like tent cabins, Big Basin has some of the best in the West. If you haven't stayed in one of these elegantly simple, comfortable and affordable wonders, make sure you try a tent cabin at least once, here or somewhere else.

▲ BIG BASIN REDWOODS STATE PARK

To get there from Santa Cruz, go north for about a dozen miles on Highway 9, then head west on Highway 236; it's just shy of 10 miles to the park. From San Francisco, take Interstate 280 south, to the Highway 9 turnoff just past Los Altos Hills. Cross Skyline Boulevard, and follow Highway 9 to Highway 236. Take that road into the park. Be sure to make reservations well in advance at 800-444-7275. It costs $16 a night to camp here. Open year-round.

Memorial County Park

There's something odd about the park system in San Mateo County. I think it's the brochure. Almost everyone pictured in it looks like they're miserable. I think they want to keep outsiders out of their little secret.

The secret is this: San Mateo County is one of the rare counties that has a truly excellent park system. And Memorial is the top choice for campers.

There are still many ancient growth redwoods here, a handsome visitor center and, best of all, a bottled up creek that has one of the best old-fashioned swimming holes in the history of the world. OK, maybe the western hemisphere. You decide.

And as if that weren't enough, about 250 yards down from the "pool" there's another terrific swimming hole that gets to be about eight feet deep year-round and has a sandy beach. Beware though, the water is really cold. The highest anyone remembers it getting is 63 degrees Fahrenheit.

It's a wonderful, winding drive through the forest to get here. You'll see signs for many city camps and private retreats, remains from the days when everyone still understood what it meant to get away from it all.

This land was largely spared from the timber and tan-bark industry of the last century, and has that special feeling of being established that seems particular to the Peninsula.

Memorial was dedicated to the 52 veterans who died in World Wars I and II from San Mateo County. It's said 52 bronze plaques were placed at the foot of 52 Memorial County Park trees, but it's a mystery where they are now.

There is the handsome, old-fashioned park furniture here that comes from the days when craftsmanship and quality were the norm in American construction. Enjoy it while it lasts.

Pescadero Creek runs through Memorial Park, and is the winter home of steelhead salmon migrating upstream from the Pacific, spawning in the spring. Naturally, everything is protected.

The rangers have a great program for the kids, which they run out of the amphitheater in the woods. I don't think there's anything more fun than seeing dozens of children squeal with delight beside their mommies and daddies under the stars and redwoods on a summer night. There's a big campfire and sometimes even a nature movie or, better yet, cartoons.

Zowie!

▲ MEMORIAL COUNTY PARK

To get there, take Interstate 280 to the Highway 84 turnoff. Go west. When you cross Skyline Boulevard the road turns into La Honda Road. Keep going. Just past the town of La Honda, make a left on Pescadero Creek Road. Follow it to the park entrance, on your left. It costs $14 a night to camp here. No reservations. Open year-round.

Henry Cowell Redwoods State Park

Here you will find the perfect combination of closeness to Santa Cruz, the beaches and real mountain quiet in a deep redwood forest. This place is not hidden—it's just that Bay Area camping aficionados have been keeping this secret to themselves for years and book the sites early. You should, too.

The 1,800 acres of this well-cared-for state park have redwoods, lush canyons with cold clear streams at the bottom, open sunny meadows and even sunny hilltops with oak forests. The San Lorenzo River is still wild and untamed here, before it runs into central Santa Cruz down below.

One of the best aspects of the park lies along the river in a place where there is no formal trail system, but where hikers with sturdy shoes and a reasonable sense of adventure can easily get around.

Look on the park map for what is called the "Garden of Eden." Walk down to the water and then along the banks, hopping on granite boulders here and following trails there, for about a mile and a half to the Rincon area. These are old fishing paths and take you on a very special, even primitive, trip into the heart of the wild Santa Cruz Mountains.

Another great trip is five minutes in the car up the Felton Empire Road to Fall Creek Park, an almost forgotten place where a very clear limestone and granite creek is the contemplative heart of the 2,300-acre preserve. Roaring Camp Railroad is a good old-fashioned train ride through the Santa Cruz Mountains to right near the Santa Cruz Boardwalk. It's about 100 yards from the campground parking lot and costs $15 for a round-trip.

The Ohlone Indians lived in this land without leaving many marks, and both parks are still a refuge from the freeways, shopping malls and office parks just miles away.

There is also an abundance of poison oak in this area, as in so many untamed California backlands. It's not going to crawl out and strangle you in the middle of the night, but, as always, know what it looks like and make sure your little ones know the rhyme I was taught as a kid growing up in California: "Leaves of three/ Let me be."

▲ HENRY COWELL REDWOODS STATE PARK

From the intersection of Highways 17 and 1 in Santa Cruz, take Ocean Avenue north (the opposite of going into town). Veer right onto Graham Hill Road. Three miles up on your left you will see the park entrance. For campground reservations call 800-444-7275. It costs $18 a night to camp here. You can camp from February 15 to October 31.

27

Joseph D. Grant County Park

The South Bay is a refuge for families. Joseph D. Grant County Park is one of their sanctuaries in the middle of the booming valley. Grant started buying this sunny, oak-dotted land when he was 22 years old. When he was done, Grant had gathered more than 2,500 acres beneath the towering peaks of Mt. Hamilton. He understood the value of privacy. Grant used his considerable influence to move Mt. Hamilton Road over one-half mile to keep things quiet on his ranch. Guests like Leland Stanford and Herbert Hoover expected the best.

Grant had mansions up the Peninsula in Burlingame and in San Francisco but his heart was here, on this land. And he understood this was a deep, natural tie for all people. Grant made his money in the steam power business, but he still made time to be a member of the Sierra Club and the Save the Redwoods League.

Today, 9,522 acres of land here belong to the people of Santa Clara County. There are 40 miles of trails and 22 campsites. This is a great place to hike and to take that fat-tired mountain bike on designated trails. Helmets required.

Just 13 miles away, and about 45 minutes along the mountain road, is Mt. Hamilton's summit. The Lick Observatory is up here, run by astronomers from the University of California at Santa Cruz. There are many programs open to the public during their regular hours of 1 to 5 P.M. daily. There are tours of the facility, concerts and opportunities to view the stars through the observatory's 120-inch reflector telescope.

▲ JOSEPH D. GRANT COUNTY PARK

Take Interstate 680 to San Jose and the Alum Rock exit. Go east about five miles to Mt. Hamilton Road. Turn right. Take Mt. Hamilton about eight more miles and you'll see the entrance on your right. There are no reservations here, just first-come, first-served. It costs $8 a night. Camping allowed on the weekends in March and then every night April 1 through October 31.

Ohlone Regional Wilderness

The San Francisco Bay Area is blessed with a wide and deep and abundant mixture of open lands carefully tended by dozens of park departments. Yet there is a hole in this otherwise carefully constructed quilt. There is hardly any place you can go nearby and truly have an overnight backpacking wilderness experience. But there is at least one. This is one spot we will send you where you have to leave the car behind and get to camp the old-fashioned way.

It may be the first time you and your little ones will truly backpack together—but after this experience, it probably won't be the last. If you and yours are ready for an introduction to the real Bay Area wilderness, look no further.

There are over 10,000 acres waiting for you here, less than an hour from the Bay Bridge. When the park district called it a wilderness it was not writing ad copy. The land is so vast and wild and unspoiled it can be called nothing else.

This expanse has only recently opened after the East Bay Regional Park District convinced the less people-oriented San Francisco Water Department to let in us humble folk. The city's rationale for making the land off limits was that it was protecting the watershed above municipal reservoirs. But as the East Bay Municipal Utility District has proved for years, there is little danger in letting taxpayers walk across their own land. Even sleep on it! The fine people at the East Bay parks lobbied hard and long for you to get into this land. And what you will discover beyond these now-open gates is a spectacle indeed.

In the springtime, the wilderness is covered with such a variety of California wildflowers that some people are now arriving each year from around the nation to witness acres of golden poppies, purple lupine and crimson indian paintbrush in fields of green wild grasses and blazing yellow mustard.

The real way to truly experience its scope is to hike across the hilly and sometimes rugged land over a two-day period—you can take the full 29-mile experience or half that depending on your pleasure and ability.

There are seven backpacking campsites in the wilderness all within well-planned walking distance of each other. The bad news is no campfires are allowed. The good news is there's piped-in drinking water at each campsite. No showers, however.

The wilderness also boasts an honest-to-goodness wild waterfall, native California tule elk grazing on the slopes and golden eagles floating on thermals high above you. Ancient oaks stud the land along with huge bay laurels, madrones and California buckeyes with an early spring bloom that gives a uniquely delicate fragrance.

To cross the land you can start at either the west entrance of Sunol Regional Park near Fremont or the east entrance near Livermore. Unless you are in excellent physical condition and like jump starts, begin near Fremont and head inland. A killer climb at the other end is much better as a steep drop on your way out.

▲ OHLONE REGIONAL WILDERNESS

Off Interstate 680 just north of the I-580 interchange, take the Calaveras Road (Highway 84) exit and head east about five miles to Geary Road and take that into Sunol Park; from there you can hike into the Ohlone Wilderness. You must get a permit from the East Bay Regional Park District before you head in. Call 510-636-1684. The rangers limit the number of folks who can enjoy this experience at any one time, so you should reserve your spot as early as possible. It costs $5 per person per night to camp here. Open year-round.

OHLONE REGIONAL WILDERNESS

Sunol Regional Park

I'm a Bay Area kid. I spent most of my waking hours outside in the rolling hills behind our old red ranch house, which was comfortably, if modestly, placed between a chicken ranch and an apple orchard. The orchard had an old barn, windmill and farmhouse owned by Mr. and Mrs. Ekes.

I still think of them when I go down to Sunol Regional Park, where the rangers have kept up the old farm and ranch buildings. You and your kids can still see the way folks lived here way back when. It's easy-going, small and good-humored, designed by the great people who work at the East Bay Regional Park District.

Here's the best part: When you get through at the exhibits and the trails and the vast views of San Francisco Bay from the ridges, you can nestle down in one of the few but extremely pleasant campsites. You will be a stone's throw away from a generous stream called Alameda Creek. It's the very same creek for which the county is named.

There's a canyon in the park called "Little Yosemite," which is sort of ridiculous because it doesn't look a thing like Yosemite. But it *is* really beautiful, especially in late spring when the grass is green, the wildflowers are out in force and the trails are dry.

Alder, willow and sycamore are evident, although not as abundant as the oaks and bay laurel and madrones.

Sunol is superb family camping right in the middle of the Bay Area. Even in the July heat, the lush oaks above provide a canopy, shading the campground and the granite gravel along the creek.

I especially recommend this campground for fog-weary San Franciscans seeking sunny summer solace.

▲ SUNOL REGIONAL PARK

Off Interstate 680 just north of the I-580 interchange, take the Calaveras Road (Highway 84) exit and head east about five miles to Geary Road and take Geary into Sunol Park. Call 510-636-1684 for camping reservations. It costs $10 a night to camp here, plus a one-time $5 reservation fee.

Mt. Diablo State Park

I always expect a little more out of the East Bay than the rest of the region. It is the most varied, least pretentious part of the Bay Area. It upsets me that with all the lovely open land in that part of the region, there are so few truly top-shelf campgrounds.

But there is always Mt. Diablo.

Word is they named this mountain after hearing the Native American legends about the origin of the earth and the powers of the spirits that fly to the remote magnificence of this place. We have taken away much of the mystery of this mountain: You can drive to the new museum at the summit, and vulgar-looking satellite relay dishes obscure the peak. But a night almost 4,000 feet above the Diablo Valley and the Bay Area brings us back to the true heart of this immense sculpture of earth.

There are several campgrounds on Diablo. I suggest you stay at Juniper, the best of the lot. It has expansive views, a reasonable amount of privacy and, at night, stargazing without peer in the Bay Area.

From the peak, on a truly clear day, you can actually see the Pacific Ocean to your west, and the Sierra Nevada to your east. In fact, it is said that you can see parts of 35 of California's 58 counties. The park rangers say the only view that surpasses Mt. Diablo's is at the top of 19,000-foot-high Mt. Kilimanjaro in Africa.

On the mountain itself, I suggest visiting the sandstone formations and caves of Rock City and the trail through Mitchell Canyon on the north side.

The campsites are all first-come, first-served. But the rangers swear there are nearly always sites available.

It took one or two million years to make Mt. Diablo. You can get there in an hour and have a California experience you will remember for a lifetime.

▲ MT. DIABLO STATE PARK

To get into the park, get on Interstate 680 through the San Ramon Valley in Contra Costa County. Take the Diablo Road exit and head east toward the mountain. Follow the signs right into the park. It costs $16 a night to camp here. No reservations. Open year-round.

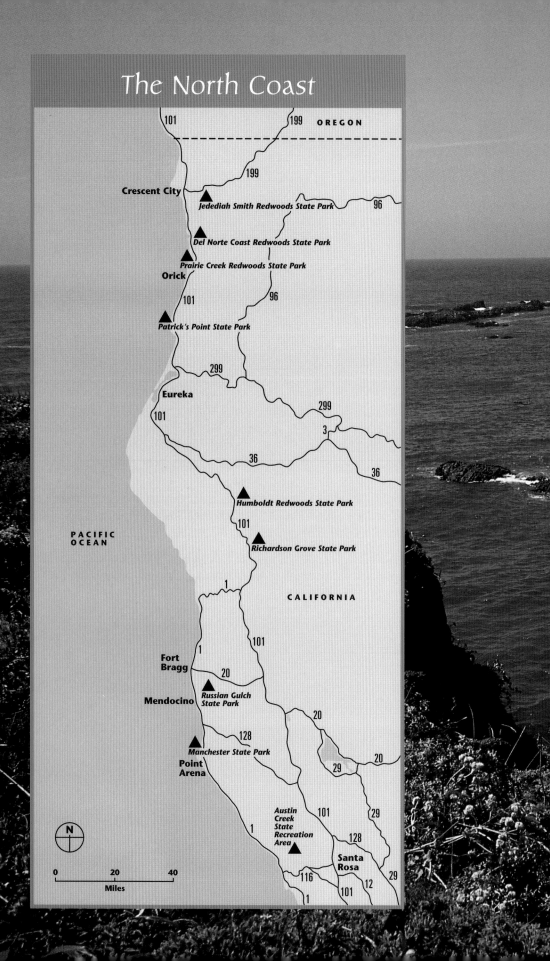

The North Coast

101   199   OREGON

199

Crescent City ▲
Jedediah Smith Redwoods State Park   96

▲
Del Norte Coast Redwoods State Park

▲
Prairie Creek Redwoods State Park
Orick
101   96

▲
Patrick's Point State Park

299

Eureka
101   299

3

36   36

▲
Humboldt Redwoods State Park
101
▲
Richardson Grove State Park

1   CALIFORNIA

101

**Fort
Bragg**
1
20   20
▲
Russian Gulch
State Park
Mendocino
128
20
▲
Manchester State Park
**Point
Arena**   29

Austin
Creek
State
Recreation   101   29
Area
▲   128
**Santa
Rosa**
116   12   29
1   101

PACIFIC
OCEAN

⊕ N

0   20   40

Miles

Del Norte Coast Redwoods State Park

This is one of the great redwood parks along the Redwood Highway where you can still find a campsite late on a summer evening. I wouldn't suggest you count on it, but I've done it before and was glad for my good luck.

First off, let's get one thing straight: It's pronounced Del Nort up here, not Del Nor-tay. If you want everyone to think you're an Auslander trying to correct the natives, that's up to you.

The redwoods are obviously the main theme here, but Del Norte has another native, too often overshadowed by its ancient neighbor. Western rhododendrons are in abundance along the coast and love to show off in this 6,400-acre preserve.

Along with azaleas, the flowers bloom best in May and June, adding buckets of vivid color.

The lumber companies had their way with this land, especially after 1908 when the railroad came in, making it easy to haul away the never-logged-before redwood forest. The line shut down in 1939, but you can see the remains of the right-of-way along the Trestle Loop

Trail. The tracks themselves were ripped up and recycled during World War II.

Despite the logging years, only one-third of the park is secondary growth; the other two-thirds is old growth. The rangers are proud of their more than eight miles of wild coastline.

Mill Creek Campground is the place to stay here. People often forget this is California's rainforest and bring just shorts and sunblock. If you make that mistake, Mill Creek may be your best rescue route because it's farther west, higher and drier than much of the surrounding area.

▲ DEL NORTE COAST REDWOODS STATE PARK

Seven miles south of Crescent City off Highway 101. Call 800-444-7275 for reservations. It costs $16 a night to camp here. Open for camping year-round.

Prairie Creek Redwoods State Park

Here it is. Heaven. OK, maybe not *the* Heaven, but a prototype. This is sort of a test Heaven, where they see how humans react to a paradise reserved for only the very lucky and the very good. Also for people willing to get off the highway.

This huge state park gets passed by all the time—it doesn't get the kind of word-of-mouth advertising that Jed Smith or Patrick's Point does. Those people who are fortunate enough to hear about Prairie Creek often come to see the herd of wild Roosevelt elk, which like to graze right near the park headquarters.

And for folks who take the trouble to do a little hiking, you may find the Pearly Gates are actually made of virgin redwood and primeval ferns.

The walk out to the coast from the Elk Prairie campground is about five miles along creeks, beside thousand-year-old trees and into the heart of the deep quiet. Every once in a while you will find people stopping on the trail, looking sort of dazed by the intensity of it all.

When you get out to the Fern Canyon Loop trail, you will have arrived.

On either side of the path there are 50-foot walls of giant ferns, much like the ones that were alive when dinosaurs roamed North America. Make sure you are wearing good footwear, in case it's wet. When you get to the beach and ocean you may never want to return.

Being a mountain biker, I was thrilled to see bikes are allowed along the perimeter trail of Prairie Creek. If you are not a biker, don't be discouraged from coming here. I know there are some extremely rude people on bikes: I've seen plenty and even once witnessed a guy on his mountain bike almost cream a toddler holding hands between his mom and dad on a trail near Tiburon. But remember that abusive bike riders are rare and should not keep you away from this most inspirational place.

▲ PRAIRIE CREEK REDWOODS STATE PARK

Off Highway 101 near Orick, look for well-marked signs for Prairie Creek. Call 800-444-7275 for reservations. It costs $16 a night to camp here. Open year-round.

Patrick's Point State Park

This favorite place is as family friendly as you will find in the Redwood Empire. It's large enough, 640 acres, with lots of campsites. The campground has a covered cook shelter, where you can feel like our very distant ancestors, making a meal with your whole community.

The kids will be climbing around the huge boulder in the middle of the park, or playing near tidepools on the beach, or running along (do kids ever walk?) across the many trails.

Then there's the Yurok Village. The park rangers dedicated this replica of a native Californian community, built in large measure by the remaining Yurok people, in 1990. There are family-sized homes, a sweat house and ceremonial structures. This village is a long-held dream. The first plans for it were drawn in the 1920s.

There is also a native plant garden worth experiencing.

Whale-watching is a favorite pastime along the many points at Patrick's Point State Park. Although it is in the redwood country, the park is rather wide open, and doesn't have a lot of redwood groves.

The 124 family campsites are generously large, and it's a short hop to the cute postcard town of Trinidad nearby.

▲ PATRICK'S POINT STATE PARK

Off Highway 101, just about 25 miles north of Eureka. Signs on the road are clear. Call 800-444-7275 for camping reservations. The price is $16 a night. Open year-round.

Humboldt Redwoods State Park

It's sometimes said the smell of redwoods has a special magic. It's as if a great power is brewing here. There are over 100 miles of paths through Humboldt Park, and the rangers will cheerfully help you find the one for you. Some trails are very easy and will take you into much of the verdant voodoo. Others are more ambitious but will take you deep into the heart of the sorcerer's kitchen.

Inside this huge (52,000 acres) park is a place called Rockefeller Forest, a 10,000-acre chunk of untouched redwoods. Yes, the Rockefellers did bestow some of their great wealth on California, and this is a tribute to some of it.

One of the reasons redwoods can live so long is tied to the reason they got their name. The "red" comes from a high level of tannin in the bark, which serves as a powerful defense against disease and insect invasions. The thick, if soft, bark also is a fire wall of sorts against the flames that naturally roar through forests in the course of time.

This park was established in 1921 after Californians began to truly understand and appreciate the redwood forests that were then getting cut down far faster than they are today. The Save the Redwoods League made the first purchase possible.

In Founders Grove, you will find some of the tallest trees on earth, trees taller than the Statue of Liberty.

▲ HUMBOLDT REDWOODS STATE PARK

Just south of the town of Weott, off Highway 101. You can't miss the many signs and several entrances. Call 800-444-7275 for reservations. It costs $16 a night to camp here. Camping season is year-round.

Richardson Grove State Park

There are three separate campgrounds in this sylvan sanctuary. I suggest you choose Huckleberry because it's under the big trees and has the most generous spaces of all the sites. Beside that, I've always been partial to the name.

Every August, just about a mile up from here, is the annual reggae festival. Don't even think of just driving up on a whim and getting a campsite then. This is one hugely popular event. If you like the music, make plans and be there. It's not a good place for a guy like Bill Clinton, however, at least if he wants to breathe or otherwise inhale. That ain't campfire smoke you're smelling.

For the fresh air crowd, I strongly recommend the first thing you do before striking out along the many redwood trails of the region is taking a short drive along the Avenue of the Giants, a road that parallels the highway but swings right through a great ancient stand of redwoods. It will whet anyone's appetite to get out of the car and march one-on-one through the forest itself.

There's also a fine old swimming hole in the park, one of the last vestiges of the Richardson heydays in the 1950s, when the park had an open-air dance floor. The purists ripped that out and all I can say is, it's a shame.

For the young—and young at heart—you will be pleased to know that you are very near one of the tackiest, most fun and certainly most loved landmarks in California: the drive-through tree. Get your cameras ready. How can you be a kid growing up in this state and not get a chance to drive through a redwood tree so big it has a car-sized tunnel at the base? Memories guaranteed.

▲ RICHARDSON GROVE
STATE PARK

About 15 miles north of Legget and south
of Redway along Highway 101. I'm partial
to Redway, a town about as pretty as people
can make them. Call 800-444-7275 for
camping reservations, which will cost you
$16 a night. Camping is year-round.

RICHARDSON GROVE
STATE PARK

Russian Gulch State Park

Remember Mendocino? That craggy, windswept spot along the North Coast where the sun and sea scoured your soul and left you ready to see what's important and what's not?

Remember when you went there last time and spent hundreds of dollars on two nights at a bed and breakfast where you had to sit around some table with a bunch of strangers scarfing up a small croissant and coffee in a tiny cup with a French name? Then you spent the whole day walking around the town, which has turned into an outdoor shopping center twice as expensive as the more comfortable indoor one in your own burg.

Now try Mendocino again the real way. Russian Gulch State Beach.

Just north of the town of Mendocino, it's the place for people who really love the true savage beauty of the region. There is a very warm family feel to this canyon, even on a cool Mendocino morning.

From here you can go into town and spend the money you didn't blow on that bed and breakfast. You can stroll right down to the beach where plenty of kids get the fresh salty spray they will never forget.

You can bike the trails, take short drives around the region and build a roaring fire at night with the waves crashing in the distance.

You can once again remember Mendocino as it is.

▲ RUSSIAN GULCH STATE PARK

Two miles north of Mendocino, right off Highway 1. Call 800-444-7275 for reservations. It costs $16 a night to camp here. Open to camping April 1 through October 11.

Manchester State Park

There is a California fantasy you may have had many times. It's the one where you take a road trip along Highway 1, traveling along the edge of the world, reveling in the beauty of the wide bluffs that run out to the seemingly infinite blue waters of the Pacific. On one particularly spectacular stretch of land between the road and the sea there are round, low hills covered with a lush carpet of wildflowers, soft green paths that lead you to sand dunes and an empty beach that runs wide and long along the ocean.

Hardly anyone knows about this place in your fantasy—it is wide open and all yours. Your children run along the surf for hours laughing with delight. As the sun begins its burning descent into the west, you light a small fire, knowing you can sleep under the stars while lulled by the distant sound of the waves crashing ashore.

The place is real. It's called Manchester State Beach. For the life of me, I don't know why it is so unknown.

If you are lucky enough to experience this spot on a sunny day, you will never forget its grandeur, its vast, dark sand beach dotted with bleached-white driftwood, its trails of green carpet snaking through lush wildflowers.

If the weather is foggy, as it is so often along the North Coast, who cares? A blazing fire, steaming pots of hot coffee and someone you love ready with warm arms will remind you to be grateful for being alive.

Manchester State Beach is very near Point Arena, that place the weather forecasters always use as a point of reference. The Point Arena lighthouse is here and a very cool side trip, just minutes away.

It's hard to say enough about this place. In case you haven't stopped to think about it, that fantasy road trip of yours has meaning. Work out the metaphors and metaphysics while you scan the ocean's horizon, sifting the sands through your fingers.

▲ MANCHESTER STATE PARK

Off Highway 1 to the west, seven miles past Point Arena in southern Mendocino County. Call 800-444-7275 for reservations. It costs $16 a night to camp here. Open year-round.

Austin Creek State Recreation Area

For a relatively quick escape from the city, old-time Bay Area families have long decamped to the Russian River. If you are a member of the ruling class, you go to the Bohemian Grove. If you earn your money the old-fashioned way, you go to Austin Creek State Recreation Area.

The park is right above Guerneville and next to Armstrong Redwoods State Recreation Reserve, where you can't camp but you can take long strolls through forests and along ridgetops and streams. It's a very short hop down to the river where you can swim at cool places like, well, Roland's Beach.

The Russian River is not for everyone. There is very little pretension. It's still wonderfully unvarnished—the object of most days here is getting a good spot on a sandy beach, tubing slowly in the water and wondering what flavor beer you'll have with your steak dinner.

You could also leave the campfire behind one evening and drive west to Occidental and Tomales and see some of the prettiest parts of the known world. If you like pasta, arrive in Occidental hungry because there are several family-style Italian restaurants in town. That's a Bay Area tradition you should take part in at least once.

▲ AUSTIN CREEK STATE RECREATION AREA

Take 116 to Guerneville and go north at Armstrong Woods Road, up three miles to the campground. No trailers here; the roads are too narrow. No reservations, just first-come, first-served. Camping costs $12 a night. Open year-round.

The Central Coast

San Jose

280

17

9

35

9

17

1

101

5

152

152

5

Santa Cruz

1

152

101

MONTEREY BAY

156

101

Monterey

68

Carmel

▲ Bottcher's Gap

1

101

Andrew Molera State Park ▲

▲ Pfeiffer Big Sur State Park

1

PACIFIC OCEAN

Kirk Creek ▲

▲ Plaskett Creek

101

Cambria

46

Paso Robles

46

1

N

0   10   20

Miles

Morro Bay

Bottcher's Gap

If you read Henry Miller novels while you were bumming in Paris during your college years, you might want to see the kind of area he gave up all that for. The drive to Bottcher's Gap from Highway 1 says it all.

Along the road you will see dreamy, woodsy homes and cabins, smoke lazily rising from the chimneys, people in plaid flannel shirts driving old trucks and yelling after some Labrador retriever called Cider. Cider will be wearing a kerchief around the neck. The dog's hipper than you.

The winding canyon road ends at this sunny inland Big Sur site. This is a small campground, just 11 sites. The ones in the far back are superior to the ones toward the front.

Here's the real story behind Bottcher's Gap: It's a portal into the Ventana Wilderness, a huge area where even the most experienced outdoorsy types say they want to explore but haven't gotten around to. Too bad.

If you ever wonder what central, coastal California looks like—I mean really looks like without any human fingerprints—the Ventana Wilderness is it. Rugged, breathtaking, immensely varied. However, take note: There is no car-camping in the Ventana Wilderness, the backpacking is very strenuous and the conditions are primitive.

At Bottcher's Gap you will be more than 2,000 feet into the sky and very comfortable.

▲ BOTTCHER'S GAP

10 miles south of Carmel on Highway 1 you will suddenly see Palo Colorado Road on your left. Follow this to the end, which is about another 10 miles. No reservations. Only $5 a night. Open year-round.

Andrew Molera State Park

Before the Vikings and the Spanish and the Yankees, native Californians lived in tiny villages along the Big Sur coast for 1,000 years. An early Spanish conquistador named it Rancho El Sur, which means "The South Ranch." The Spanish priests herded the natives into the missions system, where many died of disease and broken hearts. Shortly before the Gold Rush, an East Coast shipping captain acquired the land. He had six children, including a daughter who married a fellow named Molera.

Their descendants sold the land to the Nature Conservancy in 1968. In 1972 it once again returned to the people, 138 years after it was originally seized and fenced.

Many people rush down Highway 1 looking for Big Sur and miss this most lovely and accessible part of the land, perhaps thinking they are not in Big Sur until they see a neon sign. OK, I won't be too snotty—maybe they're looking for a hand-carved redwood sign. Maybe we should be grateful that they speed by and leave Andrew Molera State Park to us.

It is here that you can camp within strolling distance of the deep azure waters of the Pacific, where an afternoon on the beach will likely be marked by the sight of sea otters

kicking it in the kelp, the sound of seals playing in the surf and the sense that all time is meaningless and remote.

The beach itself stretches for two miles, and yes, that stream that empties out at the northern point is the Big Sur River.

Camping (tents only) is near the river just a short walk from parking at the western gate, and near the Cooper cabin, named after the Yankee ship captain.

One of my favorite spots is called the Creamery Meadow, right near Molera Point. Once dairy cows grazed here, but it has since returned to its natural wild state of great diversity. You can walk around it, watching for birds such as hawks, gulls and grubs.

The ridge trail will tempt you—go for it. And if you want to get up high and see it all, cross back over the highway and climb the slopes of the 4,800-acre park. There is a small redwood grove on one ridge and views of the world from everywhere.

▲ ANDREW MOLERA STATE PARK

21 miles south of Carmel on Highway 1, pull into the western gate. No reservations here, incredibly enough. And even better, it costs just $3 to spend the night. Open year-round.

Pfeiffer Big Sur State Park

These are the classic Big Sur camping grounds, set along the bright pure waters of the Big Sur River, covered by redwoods and alders and sycamores. Despite its size—there are over 200 campsites here—make reservations early. I've seen lots of campers here even in winter.

You are in the heart of it all here: the river, the forests, the canyons, the waterfalls. You can duck out to a great meal at the Big Sur Inn restaurant or grill your own coastal cuisine. The beach isn't far away and the park even has its own grocery store.

The most popular attraction here is Pfeiffer Falls, which are nice but not to die for. I prefer to head for Homestead Cabin, which sits on an oak-studded knoll. Manuel and Francesca Innocenti lived here and tragically lost all six of their children. Francesca lived 100 years.

There are also silly tales about supernatural spirits, like ghosts, living in these woods, which are great stories for children. You can read more in a book titled A Wild Coast and Lonely, written by Rosalind Sharpe Wall.

For a taste of comfortable luxury, I recommend dinner at the Big Sur Inn. It's also a great place to stay, if you can afford it. I'm not so keen about the Ventana Inn or the Post Ranch Inn, two enormously expensive places that are a little too slick.

▲ PFEIFFER BIG SUR STATE PARK

Almost 30 miles south of Carmel on Highway 1, you'll see the main park entrance on your left. It's open year-round and so popular you will see many tents up even in the heart of winter. Call 800-444-7275 for reservations. $16 a night.

Kirk Creek

At the southern end of the Big Sur area there is one last over-the-top coastal camp. Kirk Creek is perched right on a bluff over the Pacific, a rarity indeed in Northern California. If you like being closer inland, I suggest the Limekiln State Park campground just a few miles to the north. Limekiln is one of the newest state parks in the system and has a lot of diversity, ranging from a pretty funky beach access to much more pleasant redwood groves back in the interior.

For me, however, living right on Mother Nature's shelf over the ocean is too good to resist. You look over a small bay and across the Pacific right from your tent.

This is one of those rare situations where the national forest site is better than the state camping next door. This is also the southern end of the 1.7-million-acre Los Padres National Forest, one of the largest national forests in the nation.

▲ **KIRK CREEK**

About 35 miles south from Carmel and about 45 miles north of Morro Bay at Highway 41. Open year-round. This is one lonely stretch of road: Don't look for any towns or landmarks that can't be missed. But there are signs marking the campgrounds. Reservations are made by calling 800-280-2267. $16 a night.

Plaskett Creek

Here's a great old-fashioned campground worth visiting, especially if you are headed toward this part of the world. It's about 35 years old and feels settled in, but not shop-worn.

Plaskett Creek campground is a big loop, with the campsites arranged neatly inside the common green. Tall cypress trees give the place a nice, solid feel. The loop creates a real little town in summer, when children are running free and safe and parents are napping in chaise lounges.

If you are headed for the Central Coast, this is a great starting spot. And if you are hoping to visit Hearst Castle over a weekend, this is far superior to the state campground just south of the monument to American ostentation. Plaskett Creek is 40 miles from the publishing magnate's kingdom, and one of the prettiest 40-mile drives anywhere.

This is also a national forest site, which leads me to think that the rangers down here are unusually cool and probably inspired by the Los Padres National Forest, which includes the Ventana Wilderness.

▲ PLASKETT CREEK

This is about 45 miles south of Carmel on Highway 1 and 35 miles north of the intersection of Highways 1 and 41 near Morro Bay. Reservations are made by calling 800-280-2267. The price is $16 a night. Open year-round.

The Mountains

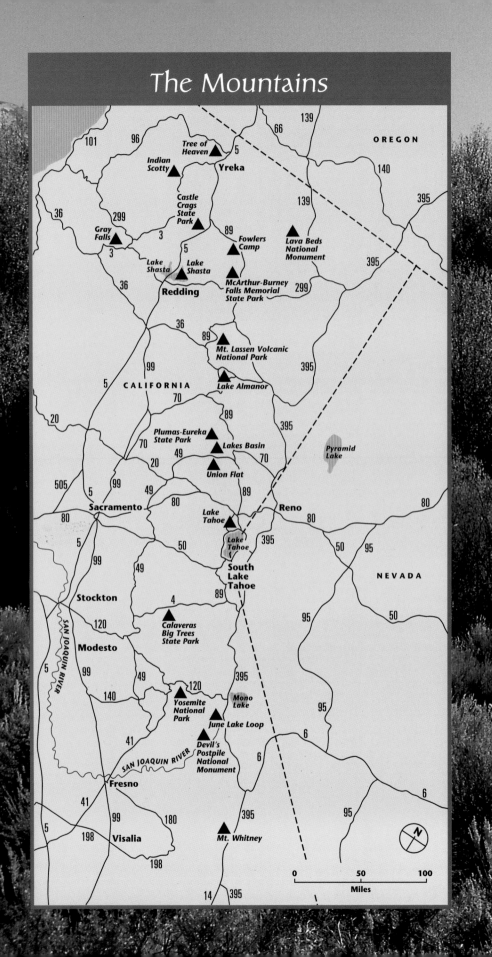

Lava Beds National Monument

Arriving here is as much of an adventure as you could ask for in California. In fact, you may well forget you are in the state, instead imagining yourself off for some exotic rendezvous in outer Mongolia. This extraordinary place is near the very top of California, almost dead-set midway between the western and eastern corners. It's reserved for the adventurous and fortunate.

There is a spartan, sunburnt spirituality to this immense valley of silence, surrounded by a ring of fire-born mountains.

Even the voyage here is special. It's a long solitary drive across a two-lane blacktop road shimmering in the sun, falling deeper and deeper into a wilderness few of us ever have a chance to truly plumb. You finally see the turnoff for the national monument and with a sweep of the hand you are rolling through a desert unlike any others you may have crossed.

As you head into the park from the south entrance, take a moment to notice the small market off to your left. I'll be sending you back there later in the day.

For right now, keep cruising up that rough paved road all the way to the official gate. Then it's a few hundred yards to the campground. Welcome.

The western junipers grow heavy here, giving you some natural shade and the kids great branches to play on. The rangers say that although the trees at the campground are shy of their 100th birthday, there are some in the park that are several hundred years old. The sites are well spaced and have that solid national park furniture that marks a first-caliber spot.

As you gaze out about the wide open landscape of gentle slopes and volcanic outcroppings you can start dreaming about the adventures that await you here. This is the true, rugged American West at the top of its form. Don't pass up the many caves here at Lava Beds. About 20 of the more than 300 are open and, literally, the coolest places in the park.

As evening falls and your eye follows the warm shadows that cover the landscape in a warm embrace, the summer heat mellows and the western sky turns a liquid orange.

On one of these evenings head back down the south road to that market you saw on the way in. It's called the Timber Mountain Store, established 1926. When you walk in you will get a heady dose of an American West gone by. The hard-worn hardwood floors, the smoke from the pool players, the boxing match on the old TV set and the classic counter where you can get a cold soda or something harder are all very special. It's something you should share with your kids, so they can see and hear and feel their past, still alive in this timeless honky-tonk.

▲ LAVA BEDS
NATIONAL MONUMENT

Take Highway 299 to Highway 139
and turn north. The entrance will
be on your left after a bit. No
reservations, $10 a night. Open
year-round.

Tree of Heaven

You know I would have picked this campground just for the name alone. But I didn't. It's a remarkable oasis unlike any other camp I've seen. Getting off the road and slipping down the slope into the campground is like opening a present that doesn't glitter until you get to the bottom of the box. Then there it is, bright and beautiful.

The tree of heaven is the literal translation of the Chinese tree we call ailanto. It is a pleasant, leafy arbor that was popular with settlers because it grows fast and well. It provides lots of shade, which in this part of the world is a nice thing to have come summertime.

The camp has lots of trees and even better still, lots of green grass rolling right down to the mighty Klamath, swiftly flowing through the high chaparral.

This is one of the best places you'll ever see for river rafting. If you have your own tube, raft or kayak, bring it here. If you don't, there are places to rent them up and down the river. Life jackets included.

You'll feel like John Wesley Powell exploring the rugged West before it was harnessed and tamed.

The drive into this National River Scenic Area is one of the best California road trips you'll ever take. The Klamath River is a wild ribbon of light in this high desert, just below the road. You speed along the smooth blacktop looking at the sunbaked land and wonder how that river got there.

For an interesting side trip, get back on the highway and head west, watching how the mountain desert suddenly turns into forest. It is abrupt and dramatic, closely following the clearly defined line where the Pacific storms stop, right about at the town of Horse Creek. After that you come to the confluence of the Klamath and Scott rivers, hugely popular with people who fish. Though there's not a decent campground nearby, it's a gorgeous day trip from the Tree of Heaven.

▲ TREE OF HEAVEN

Take Highway 96 west of Interstate 5
and enjoy the drive for 20 minutes. You'll
see the sign to make a left, taking you
down to the riverbank. First-come, first-
served. $8 a night. Open year-round.

Indian Scotty

The Scott River Valley is just fine, fine, fine. I hardly know where to begin or end rhapsodizing about this very little known area, with an unspoiled river that washes lazily over smooth granite boulders, under tall trees, along a road that gets a car about once every millennium. It's all so perfect and you have it all to yourself.

It was killing me that along the entire stretch of the Scott River there wasn't a decent campground. The sandy beaches along these pure waters, the freshness and the solitude were just too much to leave behind.

Then Indian Scotty appeared and I felt so much better.

Because it's a national forest campground there aren't the kind of amenities I prefer, for example, there are no hot showers. For some odd reason there *is* a big old swing set, but the rangers don't want to talk about it. Better to play on the maples, alders and cottonwoods.

I'm much more a river kind of person than a lake type. I can't seem to get too much of the movement of the water, the way it's always going somewhere. The life of the water is irresistible to me. The Feather, the Smith, the upper Sacramento are all world-class rivers. But I think the Scott is the best of the lot.

Head down the trail from the campground toward Jones Beach. Bring rafts, tubes, fishing gear and patience. Let the river speak to you in its native tongue. If you leave behind the noise of our language long enough, you will begin to hear something very special. A far better writer than I once said, "If not for the stones in the stream, the brook would have no song." I can't say more than that.

If you're feeling like a long drive heading south, be sure to take a stop in the tiny town of Etna. It's the kind of place you'll dream of retiring to or it will make you want to just quit your city job and raise children and apples.

▲ INDIAN SCOTTY

Take Highway 3 off Interstate 5 and head west past Fort Jones to the Scott River Road. About another 20 miles and you are there. This is a year-round, first-come, first-served campground. $6 a night.

Fowlers Camp

On the south side of Mt. Shasta is a handsome little town called McCloud, named after a gorgeous river that flows through the forests of Northern California before it dies at Lake Shasta.

You can get a good piece of this fine river at a place called Fowlers Camp. If you like the idea of catching some rainbow trout before breakfast and grilling it up for the family for the first meal of the day, this place is for you.

There are many campgrounds along this stretch of Highway 89 but Fowlers Camp is the best by far. You can fish, hike, go into town and still be close to Mt. Shasta itself.

If you're fond of waterfalls, and who isn't, there are two here, the best being Middle Falls, upstream a bit.

The Forest Service got the Upper McCloud River land in 1989 through an exchange deal with a big lumber corporation that owned it. That means we have access to 2,626 acres and 13 miles of river that were in private hands, including the falls and the beautiful Bigelow Meadow.

And while you're up in this part of the world, check out another extraordinary site: The rangers at the Shasta Trinity National Forest Service have taken an old fire lookout near Medicine Lake and made it a very special, if primitive, place to stay. It's 7,309 feet above sea level and has no piped water or electric power. It costs $35 a night. It's about an hour's drive east of Fowlers Camp. Reserved for the adventurous.

▲ FOWLERS CAMP

Take Highway 89 east from Interstate 5.
About five miles east of the town of
McCloud, you'll see the campground on
the south side of the road. Camping is
first-come, first-served. $8 a night.
Open April to November.

Castle Crags State Park

Maybe you've driven up Interstate 5 before, headed for Oregon or even Canada and finally climbed out of the Sacramento Valley and into the foothills that signal the approach of this great California landmark. To the west of the freeway they loom: huge pillars of granite, almost a gate to the country where Mt. Shasta reigns.

This is Castle Crags. These soaring spires stand by the twisting upper Sacramento River before it is dammed below. Almost 4,000 feet above you, they are about 170 million years old. And they look mighty good for their age.

This is said to be the site of the last battle between settlers and natives in which the Indians exclusively used bows and arrows to keep out the invaders. Guess who won. In 1886, the then all-powerful Southern Pacific railroad laid tracks up to Dunsmuir and that was all she wrote.

The land was opened to full-scale logging and mining. There was a time when 18 lumber mills were up and running here. Timber is still a major part of the local economy, but it's not what it used to be.

You can try walking up part of the crags, but it's an old trail, pretty well neglected in this old state park. That's really more than a shame considering its overreaching beauty and high profile. But the fantastic nature of the crags themselves, and their proximity to the Sacramento River and Mt. Shasta, make this a good camping choice. Be sure to have mosquito repellent up here.

And while you're in this neck of the woods, a side trip I really love is one to the town of Mt. Shasta, not far to the north. Head into town about two miles along the main drag, which is Mt. Shasta Boulevard, and make a left at Nixon Road. That takes you to the city park. Look for the playground and when you find it, park the car and walk across the lawn to the river on the other side. Just a few yards upstream you will see something genuinely special: the headwaters of the Sacramento River gushing right out of the earth. No kidding.

The people of this town don't seem to realize what a special thing they have here. It's almost hidden.

Then of course, there's Mt. Shasta itself, the dominating feature for the entire region, magnificently snow-capped all year long.

▲ CASTLE CRAGS STATE PARK

Off Interstate 5, take the Castella turnoff and follow the signs. It's just on the west side of the freeway. Call 800-444-7275 for reservations. $16 a night and open year-round.

McArthur-Burney Falls Memorial State Park

This a very popular park, despite its distance from the most populated parts of California. There are many folks who spend all their vacations here and are on a first-name basis with the rangers, who have seen them grow up and are now getting to know their kids.

That says two important things about the park: Making reservations far in advance is critical, and it's worth the trouble.

The major feature of this varied piece of land is Burney Falls. About 100 million gallons of water crash over this muscular cataract *every day*. The water pours out of volcanic rock above and drops 129 feet, showing off a clear blue incandescence.

This is the purest kind of water, filtered deep in the earth, not a cascading river exposed to the surface. The water seeps into the ground from snowmelt and reemerges here at a steady rate and temperature. It's really something to see.

Park rangers have very recently rebuilt much of the walkway and viewing area around the waterfall. The trail below that follows the river to the lake in the park is leafy and cool even on days when it's the surface temperature of Venus up at the top. There are also hillsides made of chalk, which will especially fascinate and delight the kids.

Lake Britton in the park is a favorite for boaters but that doesn't mean it's loud and smells like diesel fuel. Instead, the water is marked by an usually large, sandy beach, where you and yours can spend the entire day safe and sunny, swimming, making sand castles or just hanging out. You can also rent a small motorboat for a reasonable price and tour the lake. My guys loved that part the most.

More sedate and civilized families will appreciate the great bird-watching here. Bald eagles, terns, hawks and ospreys are bountiful. Migratory black swifts also draw a crowd in early summer.

One last word on McArthur-Burney: Just 30 miles away there is a very special place called Ahjumawi Lava Springs State Park, a 6,000-acre wilderness that draws a scant 2,000 people annually. That's because hardly anyone knows about it and you must have a boat to get there. Canoes and kayaks are the best because you will silently glide into this primeval setting as did ancient Californians.

▲ McARTHUR-BURNEY FALLS MEMORIAL STATE PARK

From the town of Burney on Highway 299, go northeast to Highway 89, where you go north. That will shortly take you to the park entrance on the west side of the road. Call 800-444-7275 for reservations. $16 a night to camp. Open year-round.

Gray Falls

The Trinity Alps have a strong fascination for thousands of people, I think in some measure because they are almost impossible to get into without backpacking. But you can skirt the southern end of this wilderness along the Trinity River and get great access to the back-country at this remote but very accessible camp.

Fly fishers are drawn to the trout here. Even you don't fish, the steep rocky gorges, swift water and heavy timber will more than do. In the autumn, you will find incredible colors here, even in the rock.

The handsome, old-fashioned stonework that you see in the firepits, steps and curbs make this the kind of campground you imagined as a kid.

The campground is wired for electricity but it's not up and running because they ran out of money.

Down by the river, there's a bit of sand, but not really a beach. There are tremendous boulders out into the water that call out for you to scramble across and explore. From the rocks you can look down into calm pools of water where you may see some of the biggest fish this side of the Pike Place Market in Seattle.

The falls themselves are really more like class six rapids, but a nice sight all the same.

▲ GRAY FALLS

You'll find Gray Falls on Highway 299 about 60 miles west of Interstate 5, 12 miles east of Willow Creek and 40 miles east of Highway 101. First-come, first-served. $7 a night. Open May through October.

GRAY FALLS

Lake Shasta

This immense octopus of a reservoir is somewhat intimidating. It is a boater's paradise, with endless arms of flat water under cloudless skies for days and weeks and months at a time. You can rent houseboats and speedboats here if you want to find out what that's all about.

The story of Lake Shasta is an important story about modern California. It's where the federal government bottled up the mighty Sacramento just west of Redding. It is one of the biggest dams in the world and an engineering feat that's hard not to admire.

However, more than 50 years after the dam was completed, the government guides are still defensive about the environmental criticism that haunts the project. The engineers will tell you the dam was built to stop flooding and generate electricity. They are less likely to tell you that water was harnessed for agribusiness in the Central Valley or that just about all the electricity the project generates is used to pump what's left of the water over the Tehachapi Mountains and into the thirsty Los Angeles basin.

There are hardly any rivers left in California that have escaped the control of engineers and few dams and reservoirs are as immense or as telling as this one.

Anyway you cut it, the tour inside Shasta Dam is not to be missed—a highly recommended side trip.

There are almost too many campgrounds around the lake. It would take you the better part of your vacation to check them all out not only because they are so abundant, but because they are also spread around the entire sprawling area. I recommend you go straight to Hirz Bay, where you are enough out of the way that you escape the marauding crowds but not so far away that you need a military air lift to get in and out.

You are right next to the water but also have lots of tree cover, an important plus up here where a 90-degree summer day is considered temperate.

If you like caves, be sure to spelunk your way into the Shasta Caverns. You get there on a boat ride tour across the lake that includes a good excursion along what the tour book calls "magnificent stone draperies." Can't beat that.

▲ LAKE SHASTA

Off Interstate 5, take the Gilman Road exit and head east. After 10 miles you are at the Hirz Bay campground. Reservations are made by calling 916-238-2824. $14 a night. Open year-round.

91

Mt. Lassen Volcanic National Park

Here rises one of the great peaks of the West. Named after a failed 19th-century rancher, Lassen is better known to students of California as the home of the last known Stone Age man of the United States: Ishi of the Yahi Tribe. Lassen is also well known as one of our few truly active volcanoes. Lassen last started erupting in 1914, kicking off seven years of volcanic activity still under study by geologists. It hardly looks like Mt. Saint Helens anymore, but the entire area was completely altered.

Just three years before the eruption, a man known as Ishi was driven from his bountiful land, the last human survivor of ancient America. His warm and tragic story is told very well in a classic book bearing his name. When you are on the mountain, gazing through the deep aquamarine of the permafrost, soaking in the high mountain sun and slowly savoring the deep pine forests, this is the time you will want to know about the humans who lived here for centuries before being slaughtered and chased from their ancestral lands.

There is magnificent beauty at Mt. Lassen. If you choose your campground carefully, you will experience it at its best.

I strongly recommend Summit Lake North or Manzanita Lake on the northern slopes of the mountain.

Summit is a good campground with outstanding access to a lovely mountain lake. Kids splash here in the pure waters, older folks stroll along the pine forest shores, staring across the blue-mirrored surface and off into the universe.

As for Manzanita, which is farther off and kind of in the middle of nowhere, well, it's the best. The rangers have built a little village here with a market, laundromat and even a

paperback lending library next door to the campground host. The lake is right next door to the campground. I highly recommend this special spot.

The one trip you must consider is the hike to the top of the mountain. You can park just two and a half miles below the summit and take the vigorous hike 2,000 feet up to the top. My eight-year-old did it and still crows about the accomplishment years later. So get out there and take that hill.

A quick note for people with health conditions aggravated by high altitudes: All the campgrounds are above 5,650 feet and can cause medical problems. If this is of some concern to you, check with your physician first.

▲ MT. LASSEN VOLCANIC NATIONAL PARK

Take Highway 36 east off Interstate 5. The main park entrance road will be on the north side of the road. After passing through the gate, follow the cross-park road (Highway 89) to Summit Lake North on your right side. For Manzanita Lake, continue to the north side of the mountain and the campground will be on your west. Open May through September. $10 a night and no reservations.

Lake Almanor

The first time I saw Lake Almanor I remember being startled at its size. Then I thought what an excellent place it would be to water ski. Then I began wondering why I had never heard of this place.

It's an immense body of water, created by a PG&E dam on the incredible north fork of the Feather River. It's kind of a drag that the giant utility has bottled up just about every pristine waterway in California, flooded spectacular valleys and all that. But here I am enjoying all the cheap electric power they provide me. And Lake Almanor is really very pretty.

There are several campgrounds around the lake, but be sure you hit the right one: The north/south campgrounds called Almanor 2 and 3 along the shore that have their own beach are for you.

This is the kind of vacation place to go to when you're dreaming of a comfortable chaise lounge parked along a vast lakeshore and warm dry summer breezes lulling you to sleep as you suck down a cold drink and read pulp fiction. Maybe you have a lazy summer baseball game on an old transistor radio. But no phones, no beepers, no e-mail.

You wanna go into town, there's the little resort village of Almanor itself. Great for the essentials like beer and chips.

You want something with a little more native character, head up to the northern end of the lake and get a ranch-style dinner in Chester. Buy some cowboy boots. Yahoo.

And if you are lucky enough to have a speedboat and water skis, you'll probably be doing a lot of that at Lake Almanor.

▲ LAKE ALMANOR

Take Highway 36 east off I-5.
After passing Highway 89 north
continue to where you can take
89 south, which is where you turn.
A little more than six miles down
you'll see the signs to turn left
toward the campgrounds. I advise
skipping Almanor 1. Numbers 2
and 3 have 131 sites so there's
usually lots of room. Open year-
round. Call 916-386-5164 for
reservations. $10 a night.

Plumas-Eureka State Park

Exploring places nobody goes to or even knows about has its risks. Here's the way I figure it: One in every three attempts turns into abject failure. Your family looks at you like you really are the fool they long suspected and your friends call you really rude names. One of three places is pretty humdrum and you can repeat the above reactions. And one out of every three places is like Plumas-Eureka State Park. Everyone thinks you're Neil Armstrong, Lewis and Clark and Marco Polo.

My crew was pretty beat by the time I had driven them miles off Interstate 80. We had taken a break in the pretty outpost of Graeagle and they were tempted by the comfortable-looking motels. I pleaded with them to hang in with me. We drove into Plumas-Eureka and my family extended my contract as dad-explorer.

The park is way cool and the camping is way past cool. The sites are open and attractive, with some of the friendliest-looking family campers I've ever seen. Lots of kids on bikes zooming around under tall, mature trees and jumping off to play in a great big creek perfect for kid explorers.

Close to the entrance of the park is a compound of handsome old red barns and other buildings that house a very excellent museum, old mining equipment and the mining ruins themselves.

We were poking around the buildings after the official closing hour one warm summer evening when a ranger started strolling our way. I got ready for the great American Authority speech about it being shut down, off limits, go away. You know the drill. Instead, he said it was a shame it was closed for the night because there was all this interesting stuff inside and started to tell the kids some great stories and answer all our questions.

Way to go.

▲ PLUMAS-EUREKA
STATE PARK

Head for the town of Graeagle on
Highway 89 in Plumas County. There's
a sign for the park just on the northern
edge of town; look for County Road A14
and head west, five miles into the park.
Open May through September; call
800-444-7275 for reservations. It costs
$16 a night to camp here.

Lakes Basin

Welcome to a spot in California reserved only for the cognoscenti of camping: the Lakes Basin Recreation Area. Gold Lake, Long Lake, and the Salmon Lakes are among the many sweet spots hidden in these mountains off to the north of the Mother Lode.

There are many campgrounds here, including the newly renovated Lakes Basin Campground. We explored them all carefully and settled in at Salmon Creek, where the kids played with new-found friends along the water, building stone houses, skipping rocks and getting thoroughly soaked in the summer sun.

People were fishing in the streams and lakes, and finding wildflowers along craggy mountain trails. Some folks explored the many lakeside lodges. Others drove over to the idyllic town of Graeagle to golf. If you like picture-perfect little towns as much as I do, take a little time to see nearby Calpine.

We took our boys on a hike they will remember and brag about when they are 100 years old. Starting near Packer Lake, we marched along sun-washed granite buffeted by crimson,

gold and indigo wildflowers up to the Sierra Buttes, an outcropping of rock that can be seen from hundreds of miles around the Mother Lode.

We stopped to eat along an alpine lake, threw snowballs along the ridge in the middle of August, and made the final ascent to a fire tower at the top of the buttes—a place that is honestly beyond imagination.

This is truly an ignored part of California, and we can all be thankful for that. I suspect in 20 years people will be saying, "Yeah, we used to camp at the Lakes Basin in the '90s! That's when you didn't need reservations and it cost next to nothing."

Thanks, Gramps.

▲ LAKES BASIN

Take Highway 49 to Bassetts. You'll see
a store on the north side of the road,
which is the corner of Gold Lake Road.
Go north here and in a few miles you'll
see the Salmon Creek entrance on your
left. A little farther up the road, you'll
see Lakes Basin Campground. No reservations. $6 a night. Open June through
October.

Union Flat

Highway 49 is a justifiably popular drive in California. It takes you into the heart of the gold country, along a very pretty river and into some of the most handsome and historic towns of the West.

Toward the bottom of this stretch of road is Nevada City, a sort of ersatz Carmel in the Sierra foothills. But rising above the town is the fabled land where miners actually scraped and panned and killed for the 19th-century version of the California lottery.

There are relatively few quality campgrounds along this historic stretch of Highway 49, but the one I choose is Union Flat. It enjoys privacy, isn't too crowded, has minimum road noise and, best of all, it's right on the Yuba River.

When you're ready to do a small road trip and explore the region, here are my top picks: Downieville and Sierra City will make the parents happy with their mountain charm; the kids will love the Feather River Railroad Museum up in the Sierra Valley, California's own true altiplano. There is also the Kentucky Mine, a great old gold mine now open as an outstanding exhibit.

You can still pan for gold up here—and some people find it. The Gold Rush ended, not because the gold ran out, but because the 49ers (the original, real ones) got greedy and almost destroyed the rivers by washing the soils downstream with huge, steam-powered hoses, eroding away entire mountainsides in search of riches.

When the bed of the Sacramento River finally got too high because of the debris, the state capital flooded and the state legislature said enough. Hydraulic mining ended, the Gold Rush was over and the land was left to become a place for quiet relaxation.

▲ UNION FLAT

On Highway 49, about five
miles east of Downieville. The
gate will be on your south side.
No reservations, $8 a night;
open May through October.

Lake Tahoe

Growing up in the Bay Area, I was long under the impression that Tahoe was for fat-cat San Franciscans. I thought you had to motor in with your friends in a convertible German sedan and stay at an elegant lakeside lodge built of timbers, kind of like the Ponderosa with a snotty attitude. Hot toddies and all that.

Some of the best real estate along the lake, in fact, belongs to you. You can truly enjoy your land along Emerald Bay, Sugar Pine Point and elsewhere. There are wonderful choices here—and a few places to avoid.

Lake Tahoe is far wider than a church door, and considerably deeper than a well. The 37 trillion gallons of high Sierra water is enough to cover all of California 14 inches deep. It is the 10th deepest lake on the planet, reaching down 1,645 feet into the earth.

The water is very clear and very cold. The snows from the mountains ringing the 71-mile shoreline melt all year long into the lake. Tahoe's only natural outlet is the Truckee River, which runs inland into the vast Pyramid Lake of the Nevada desert.

The California shore is the place to watch the sunrise break over the eastern mountains, setting the lake before you into a cold fire of orange and blue. A pot of hot coffee, a pan of smoky bacon and some thick slices of warm bread will be the beginning of a great day.

At night, the shooting stars above the water at 6,225 feet elevation are a sight indeed.

There are many campgrounds along the shores of Tahoe and many more a short drive from the lake. But three are truly the best by a long shot: Bliss, Sugar Pine and Emerald Bay. These are all California state parks that offer cleanliness, safety and comfort. I strongly advise you to avoid the national forest campgrounds in the area, which like so many of this agency's sites, are scraggly afterthoughts to clear-cutting, strip-mining and dirt-bike riding.

There is one more site very near Tahoe, just minutes away really, that I highly recommend, especially if you want to get away from the busy lakeshore. Fallen Leaf Lake is itself a spectacular, if not overscale, blue jewel in the Sierra. The campsites are generously large, with walking trails through the pine forests to the lake and next-door Mount Tallac, a dramatic peak too often forgotten.

Generally speaking, the farther inland you go at these campgrounds, the more privacy you get. At inland Bliss, for example, you get great granite boulders that kids love to scramble over. The closer you get to the shores of Tahoe itself, the closer you are to this immense lake of clarity and scope, but you are also getting a little less space and a little more noise.

Sugar Pine seems a little rowdier than the other two, but is nicely situated. Bliss seems to have the most room. Emerald Bay is probably my current favorite because it's right along that beautiful cove.

▲ LAKE TAHOE

Sugar Pine, Emerald Bay, and Bliss campgrounds are directly off Highway 89 between South Lake Tahoe and Tahoe City. The turnoff for Fallen Leaf Lake Campground is on Highway 89, a couple of miles north of Tahoe City. Sugar Pine is open year-round; Emerald Bay, June through September; and Bliss, June through October. Call 800-444-7275 for reservations. $16 a night. Fallen Leaf Lake is open May through September. Call 800-280-2267 for reservations, which are $16 a night.

LAKE TAHOE

Calaveras Big Trees State Park

The celebrated frog jumping contest of this county takes place down the road from here at Angel's Camp, about 30 minutes away.

As for the park itself, you don't have to be a rocket scientist to know what the big attraction is here. Rhymes with bees. Big bees.

The giant sequoias are quite a sight. It's easy to get into them and stroll gently across this soft forest floor, filling your lungs with that wonderful scent and gazing up at these extraordinarily tall stands of timber.

There are two well-defined groves of trees, one to the north, the other to the south. The north is the more popular but the south is far larger and more varied.

The *Sequoiadendron giganteum* is a member of the last man club, or last tree species club. Giant sequoias are one of a few remaining members of a botanical family that includes the dawn redwood of China and the famous coastal redwood of Northern California. As a species, these giant sequoias are experts at survival: They were alive and prospering when the dinosaurs were eating forests for lunch.

You are also near the Stanislaus River and Beaver Creek, and a well-developed trail system can take you to just about anywhere you care to experience in the area, including stunning mountain streams with round granite boulders, pure mountain waters and abundant California sunshine.

If you hanker for a trip into town, the nearby village of Arnold is as pretty as can be—a neat country town where the living is easy.

There are two campgrounds in Calaveras Big Trees and either one will more than do, but I recommend Oak Hollow over North Grove Campground.

▲ CALAVERAS BIG TREES STATE PARK

Take Highway 4 from Angel's Camp and head east for about 25 miles. Right after you go through Arnold, the park is on the south side of the road. Reservations can be made by calling 800-444-7275. $16 a night. Open year-round.

Yosemite National Park

One of the most celebrated places on God's green earth, Yosemite attracts millions of people each year from around the globe. And with good reason. I challenge anyone not to gasp when they first enter the valley floor, passing El Capitan, Yosemite Falls and Half Dome.

Ironically, one of the most popular places to stay here is a cheesy-looking motel, which all but desecrates the land.

On the other hand, there is the lovely Ahwahnee Hotel, but one night's lodging can cost you enough to pay for your own national park in some countries.

That, naturally, brings us to the camping. Let me summarize the situation on the crowded valley floor in two words: it sucks.

However, there is, thankfully, Bridalveil Creek campground.

You will find this wonderful bit of Yosemite above the valley, along a stream and away from the tour buses but close to one of the best views in North America and very much in the heart of the real Yosemite.

Half a billion years ago this land lay beneath an ancient ocean. Forces beneath the earth's mantle began forcing it to the surface, with deep plumes of molten stone forming granite. Water, glaciers and other forms of erosion sculpted the land as we know it today.

We also know that 100 years ago a loner named John Muir walked from places as far away as his home in the East Bay town of Martinez all the way to Yosemite. His writings, his lobbying and his all-consuming passion for the mountains led to the creation of Yosemite National Park.

Because of him, your children can climb up to the foot of waterfalls. What's more, they can see how native Californians lived on the valley floor and get a wonderful overview of the entire place at the excellent museum.

When you are camping at Bridalveil Creek, be sure to head down the road a bit to Glacier Point for a view of the valley floor that may stun you.

It's said that on a full moon night, the sight of the valley from Glacier Point will make you howl.

If you are in half-decent condition, you can stroll all the way down to the valley, during the day, of course. Bridalveil Falls is some distance, so be sure to check your maps and ask lots of questions before you start off exploring the park.

▲ YOSEMITE NATIONAL PARK

To get to Bridalveil Creek, you enter the park on
Highway 140. As you drive into the valley itself,
you'll soon see a turn to your right called Glacier
Point Road. You still have 25 miles to go, but it's
a drive you'd do just for sheer pleasure. (Coming
back down has even better views.) The campground entrance will be on your right, just as
you cross over the creek. Camping is open June
through September with no reservations. Just
first-come, first-served. $10 a night.

June Lake Loop

The eastern Sierra Nevada is one of the most hidden yet fabulous areas of California. Some people venture out to Mono Lake, a few others love the drive down U.S. 395. In fact, they love it so much hardly anyone pulls off the road at the June Lake Loop and spends time in the fresh, remote high desert.

The road takes you right up the cliffs that soar into the Sierra Nevada. Jagged granite peaks with snow much of the year provide lots of fresh water for the lakes below.

There are three principal lakes. Since most people can't be in more than one place at one time, Silver Lake is the single best choice here. There's a large campground running right up to the water, a decent boat ramp and in the final analysis, it's just the best-looking place of the bunch.

The nearby resort town of June Lake has all the stuff resort towns usually have: a laundromat, restaurants, drug stores and bars.

The entire area has a way-out-of-the-way feel that's at once kind of lonely and kind of peaceful.

If you feel like taking a gander at the town and June Lake in one glance, follow the road as it keeps looping toward 395. At the top of the rise you'll be on a ridge with the unlikely name of "Oh! Ridge." Makes me wanna holler gosh and golly just thinking about it. There's a campground here, but it's no big deal. The view is good; the breeze will make you think of all the great windsurfing on the lakes.

▲ JUNE LAKE LOOP

Off Highway 395, a little more than 10 miles south of Lee Vining. You'll see the sign for the loop road on the west side. No reservations, $10 a night, open from mid-April through October.

Devil's Postpile National Monument

This little-visited wonderland is hidden behind the huge and hugely popular Mammoth Lakes ski resort area. The gates to the monument are closed in the winter when most visitors are here. Mountain bikers love Mammoth for the rugged trails in summer.

The camping here is pretty good but the campground at the next-door national forest Minaret Falls site is also attractive. The rangers at Devil's Postpile National Monument point out that their sites are better patrolled and feel safer than the national forest site.

A most incredible thing at Devil's Postpile is the river running right by the campgrounds. It's pure and clean and very beautiful. I was blown away when I checked the map and saw it's the San Joaquin River, a waterway I usually associate with Central Valley agribusiness, toxic amounts of selenium and general ruination.

Here, the river is just eight miles from its headwaters and dazzling.

The single most tremendous aspect of the park is the postpile itself. It's not all that big, but it's truly a marvel to see.

The trail down from the campground is just a half mile or so and pleasant. A bit farther along there's Rainbow Falls, splashing down 101 feet from a cliff of volcanic andesite and rhyodacite.

There was a nasty fire in this area in 1992, but things seem to be recovering nicely now.

If you're tent camping instead of in a trailer or RV, be sure to have good padded groundcover. Lots of the sites are pretty rocky.

But then, rock is what this place is all about. The stunning columns of volcanic basalt were formed about 100,000 years ago. That's a blink in geologic time. You can hike to the top of the formation and see a cross section that looks like a kitchen floor.

If you miss Devil's Postpile here in California, don't worry. You can see similar freaky formations in Ireland, Scotland and Australia. But I can't say much about the camping.

▲ DEVIL'S POSTPILE NATIONAL MONUMENT

On Highway 395, go 26 miles south of Lee Vining and take the Mammoth exit to the west. Go past the Mammoth ski resort and follow the signs to the national monument. No reservations, just show up and pay the $8. Open June through October.

Mt. Whitney

I almost had a pretty decent news story up here. While I was scanning a topographical map of the area with a ranger, he implied Mt. Whitney was not the highest peak in the 48 contiguous states. White Mountain on the other side of the Owens Valley was, he strongly suggested. But everyone was keeping hush-hush, because losing Whitney's top distinction would dry up tourist dollars, make every tour guide in the world wrong and just generally make the science community look silly.

After half a dozen phone calls I found the rumor's source and spiked it. Mt. Whitney still rules and beats White Mountain by a few hundred feet. Phew.

Anyway, you can't drive up close to the top of White Mountain and hike to the peak like you can at Whitney. That's an 11-mile experience and an accomplishment you shouldn't miss, especially if you consider yourself a real Californian.

The road connecting U.S. 395 to the high country parking lot is very special. Have the camera handy as you're going up, and pull off to the right when you see the historic

marker. You will learn that these dramatic, rocky slopes are called the Alabama Hills and have been the site of hundreds of movies and TV westerns. Tom Mix, Roy Rogers, John Wayne and Humphrey Bogart all filmed here.

The sandstone and granite boulders made a great location for shootouts, hideouts and blowouts.

If you want to camp at the top of the road, there's a very nice, if somewhat cramped, campground right at the trailhead. The rangers have made elevated beds of crushed stone for a comfy night under the pines and stars. A high-quality, year-long stream rushes nearby, making beautiful night music.

The view of the Owens Valley below is still another bonus, but one you also can get down a bit lower at the spacious Lone Pine campground, another highly recommended spot in the high desert wilderness.

▲ MT. WHITNEY

On Highway 395, go to Lone Pine, then go west on Whitney Portal Road. It ends at the parking lot where you can camp and start up the 5,400-foot rise in elevation to the summit. The Lone Pine campground will be on the left side of the road before you get to the end. Reservations for both can be made by calling 800-280-2267. $10 a night. Open year-round.

Central California

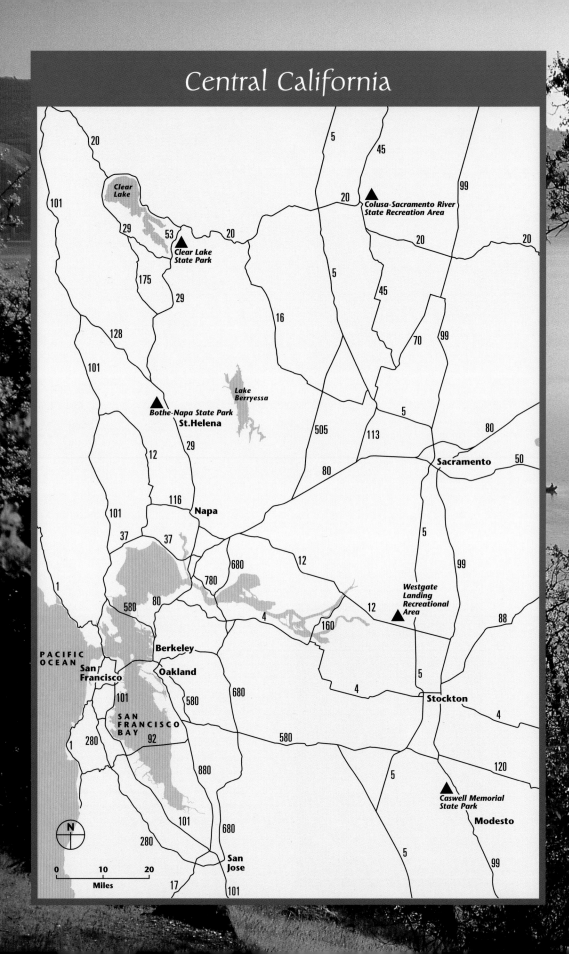

Caswell Memorial State Park

To understand the real California, you must know and respect the heart of our state: the great Central Valley.

And what's not to love in our heartland?

The sight of poplar trees melting with gold in the autumn twilight along a two-lane blacktop framed by wild sunflowers? Corn fields for miles and miles, the sweet white kernels ripening behind a blond shock in the husk? Wild blackberries as big as figs and black mission figs as big as apples sweetening in the summer heat by a slow river?

Caswell is a special California spot on a lazy stretch of the Stanislaus River. It has a wide, sandy beach where you can throw in a tube or a raft or a fishing line. The campsites are generous and private under the valley oaks, thriving in the deep topsoil of this astonishing land. The amber light from your fire will blot out the stars—but when the embers burn down and the crickets call you to sleep, the constellations will stun you with clarity.

A few things you should know: You can't get away with forgetting your mosquito repellent here. They get as big as vampire bats and are twice as thirsty. This a good spot on the way to someplace: Yosemite, Tahoe, points north and south on Interstate 5, but may not be a destination for everyone. You will tend to see campers driving well-cared-for family pickups from Hayward, not Volvos from Berkeley. Remember, this is the heartland.

▲ CASWELL MEMORIAL STATE PARK

Two miles south of Manteca on Highway 99 take the Austin Road turnoff and go south another four miles to the park. Call 800-444-7275 for reservations. $16 a night. Open year-round.

Westgate Landing Recreational Area

I love the Delta. It is California's under-explored and underappreciated heart of water and sun. High above the fruit orchards, levee roads twist and bend gently, showing you this wonder and that marvel for more than 100 square miles where the mighty Sacramento and San Joaquin rivers meet before taking their joint journey to San Francisco Bay and out the Golden Gate.

My ideal spot in the slow-moving Delta would be an unassuming grassy plain, within strolling distance of a hidden waterway where a small dock awaits you and yours.

Westgate Landing is as close to that ideal as I have found.

The evening I first arrived at this little-known spot, a young couple was quietly basking in the late afternoon sun, he in the water holding onto the dock, she sitting on the warm boards, feet in the water, looking down on his water-splashed face.

In the morning, you awake to the smell of the fresh corn field next door, the sweet waters of the bayou on the other side of the small campground and songbirds celebrating the sparkling new day.

There are serious blackberry bushes here. The Delta heat and moist peat soils make for some of the richest growing earth on the planet. Late July and almost all of August are primo picking times. You can go crazy.

If you have a boat, the free launch is for you.

If you can appreciate a simple, clean and earthy camp, Westgate Landing is just right.

▲ WESTGATE LANDING RECREATIONAL AREA

From Interstate 5, take Highway 12 west for about 5 miles. Glasscock Road is on the north side in the "town" of Terminous, which is your turn. Drive north along the road about a mile, make a left and you are there. No reservations. $9 a night. Open year-round.

Bothe-Napa State Park

California's fabled wine country. There's nothing more pleasant than a day in the vineyards, in the golden hills, in the resort towns and spas. The only thing making it better is to actually sleep *in* the wine country, under the valley's bright stars, with the soft scent of the vine-country floating up to your campsite.

At the southern edge of the park you can visit a real grist mill, so the next time you use that metaphor you'll actually know what you're talking about.

Bothe-Napa (pronounced Both-ee) is definitely the best place to stay in the valley. You are central to everything: Calistoga is minutes away, the best-known wineries are all around you and best of all, this well-tended state campground has a swimming pool.

After a day of bike riding, mud-bath soaking and vineyard picnicking, you and the kids can splash away the rest of the warm afternoon. Remember, it doesn't get dark during summer until about 9 P.M.

After that, how about a bottle of wine for the grownups and hot chocolate for the kids? You all deserve marshmallows. But don't burn them!

▲ BOTHE-NAPA STATE PARK

On Highway 29, four miles north of St. Helena. Call 800-444-7275 for reservations. $16 a night. Open year-round.

Clear Lake State Park

There's no denying that many people think of Clear Lake as the kind of place you go to if you want to get in a bar fight and throw beer bottles into the back of your pickup truck on your way to the next brawl. That's unfair and untrue. The state park along the shores of this immense lake and in the oak-covered hills overlooking the water tell it all.

One balmy July evening I pulled into the campground and found the upper reaches at the Bayview sites all but empty. There was one other family of humans having a barbecue, and a small flock of wild turkeys crisscrossing the camp looking for food. Some of the little chicks were no bigger than my hand.

The sites below, on the water, were filled up. Some kids were out in the late afternoon sun getting in one last swim. A few die-hard fishers were casting last lines before heading back to grill up a catch of bass and catfish under the oaks and buckeyes.

In the morning, the sun broke over the lake, the air was cool but lovely and the hot coffee was just the way to start off. The nearby town of Kelseyville is more than easygoing, although I'm partial to Lakeport up the road a bit.

▲ CLEAR LAKE STATE PARK

From Highway 29 in Kelseyville, take the Main Street turnoff, then north on State Street, then north on Gaddy Lane, then west on Soda Bay to the park. Call 800-444-7275 for reservations. $16 a night. Sites right on the water cost more than others at peak times. Open year-round.

Colusa-Sacramento River State Recreation Area

The Central Valley has a fascinating natural history, which it has left far behind. You can recapture the true feel of this remarkable land here, on the outskirts of the charming town of Colusa, along the mighty Sacramento River.

For eons, the valley floor was a vast reservoir for the waters that washed down from the coastal hills to the west and Sierra Nevada to the east. During wet years, great swaths of the valley were submerged, while the water slowly percolated through the earth's rich surface to vast underground reservoirs below. Along with the rain and snowmelt came the top soil from the hills and mountains. The deep alluvial soil, the high water table and the abundant summer sun make for near-perfect growing conditions.

This eventually attracted big business, which began buying family parcels up and down the valley floor. They pumped enormous amounts of water out of the earth for water-intensive (and highly profitable) summer crops. But they didn't use those old-fashioned wooden windmills; they built huge diesel-driven pumps. The land began to buckle and sink and dry up at top, just as it had in the South where the dustbowls destroyed so much.

The federal government, under FDR, feared a repeat of that disaster and made a plan: Harness the great rivers of Northern California and give the water to the farmers on the promise that they would break up the big business combines and stop pumping so much water. The state did the same in the early 1960s. Unfortunately, many of the agribusiness promises were never kept.

Towns like Colusa sprang up in the glory years and have kept going very nicely with the taxpayer-subsidized water and Mother Nature's great gifts.

There's a park in the middle of this all-important California story and it's worth a visit. The river winds by slowly, having been bottled up and tamed to the north at Shasta Dam. The land is flat, dark and loamy for miles, with crops in every direction. Big lawns are kept green with the river water; shady trees and perfect conditions for bike riders beckon. Walnut groves are just around the corner.

The town itself is my favorite part of camping here. The old courthouse, the old-fashioned downtown, the county fair during the last week of June are all enough for me. You can have the best of Mother Nature's blessings and mankind's imprint.

▲ COLUSA-SACRAMENTO RIVER STATE RECREATION AREA

Off Interstate 5, go east for 20 miles on Highway 20 until you get into the town of Colusa. Get on Tenth Street and follow the signs for the park. Call 800-444-7275 for reservations. $16 a night. Open year-round.

What to Bring

Even if you have a big family van, a roof rack and a trailer, I say camping is best when you have what you *need*, not everything you can stuff in, strap down or drag along. That doesn't mean you have to play John Calvin or Francis of Assisi. Deprivation will not make you a saint or make camping fun. Comfort will. Have I just contradicted myself? Here's the key word: balance. The following checklist of what to bring is basic. You should add and subtract to suit your own needs. After every trip you will learn a little more about what to bring and leave behind for yourself. Just scribble it in here and you're set.

1. A strong, well-made pop-up dome tent that you can sleep in *and* store important stuff in at the same time, like packs. But don't leave food in your tent *ever*. Bears are everywhere.

    Even if you have a tent-trailer or RV, you might bring along a tent for the kids. I've never met a child who didn't love sleeping in one.

2. A well-made sleeping bag is a must. Spend the extra $50 and get the best. If you get cold easily, you need a zero-degree bag at a minimum. Ten degrees below or more isn't a bad idea. Remember, you'll be spending a third of your time in this. Invest wisely.

3. Groundcloth and pad. You *must* have a simple waterproof groundcloth under you and your tent. Pads come in all sizes and prices. Car campers can take comfy foam pads; some people like air mattresses. I find them a little too bouncy for my taste, but you may not.

4. Mosquito repellent. This will be the best few bucks you ever spend. Get the spray kind so you can get the outside of your clothes as well as your skin and hair. I will never ever forget one summer night many years ago when I forgot to bring the repellent. Before the first hour of twilight was over I counted more than two dozen huge bites on my forehead alone. And, naturally, don't forget waterproof sunscreen!

5. Water bottles. The quart bottles will save your life a hundred times. The best are the kind you can carry on your waist.

6. Flashlights. I like the kind you can strap on your head, leaving both hands free to get water, cook dinner and find the car keys. Kids love to have their own flashlights and will whine for hours if they don't each get one.

7. Knife. You can get one of those Swiss Army knives with every attachment in the world, a buck-knife in a holster or a big serrated bread knife. Whatever suits you. But bring a knife. Can and bottle openers are also very strongly recommended.

8. Matches. Keep them in a waterproof container such as a plastic bag or box. A lighter is even better. But keep them all away from curious little hands.

9. Lantern. The propane kind throw out the best light so you can play cards, read books or make a meal in the dark with one. The electric kind are handy but tend not to provide as much illumination. The propane cook stoves are also a great and very worthy thing to have although most campsites have barbecue pits, which is part of the fun.

10. Firewood. This may seem absurd to novice campers. You're headed into the woods, right? Guess what: Almost every park prohibits gathering wood because the large number of campers would strip the forest floor bare of this important part of the ecosystem. A lot of places sell a box of firewood for $5 but you can burn through that in an hour. It's cheaper and better to bring a big box of your own. Also a hatchet. Don't forget your hatchet!

11. Towels, both cloth and paper. You'll use these all the time.

12. First aid kit. You can get basic kits at a drug store or outdoors store, or you can assemble the basic components (aspirin, bandages, disinfectant, etc.) yourself. One special word about poison oak. Learn to recognize it, make sure your kids go through the drill of recognizing it on the trail every day and *never* touch it at any time of year. *Never* burn it; people die from inhaling the smoke. If you touch it, wash the area right away with cold water and soap. Wiping with rubbing alcohol is also very effective and easy. Symptoms show up in three to six days.

13. Cooking gear. Keep it simple and don't bring anything that you don't want dented, scratched or burned. Forks, knives and aluminum foil are a must.

14. A cooler. Life itself would be impossible without a cooler or ice chest.

15. Patience. Maybe this should be first on the list. If you are new to this, you have a small learning curve ahead of you and the kids can drive you crazy when you're trying to set up a tent in the dark for the first time. Or the tenth time. Make a pact with yourself and your family that the mission ahead is to have fun. Whenever someone stops having fun, someone *else* is breaking the pact. My kids say, "Take a chill pill and move to Brazil." But just counting to 10 and your blessings will usually do the trick.

Index